FROM PHILO
TO SPINOZA

FROM PHILO
TO SPINOZA:

TWO STUDIES
IN RELIGIOUS
PHILOSOPHY

HARRY AUSTRYN
WOLFSON

*Introduction by
Isadore Twersky*

BEHRMAN HOUSE | PUBLISHERS | NEW YORK

Library of Congress Cataloging in Publication Data

Wolfson, Harry Austryn, 1887-1974.
  From Philo to Spinoza.

  Includes bibliographical references.
  CONTENTS: What is new in Philo?—Spinoza
and the religion of the past.
  1. Philo Judaeus. 2. Spinoza, Benedictus de,
1632-1677. 3. Religion—Philosophy—History.
I. Wolfson, Harry Austryn, 1887-1974. Spinoza
and the religion of the past. 1977. II. Title.
B689.Z7W685   1977   200'.1   77-1909
ISBN 0-87441-262-5

10   9   8   7   6   5   4   3   2   1

ACKNOWLEDGMENTS

"What Is New in Philo?" from *Philo: Foundations of Religious Philosophy in Judaism, Christianity, and Islam* by Harry Austryn Wolfson. Copyright © 1947 by the President and Fellows of Harvard College. Reprinted by permission.

"Spinoza and the Religion of the Past," from *Religious Philosophy: A Group of Essays* by Harry Austryn Wolfson. Copyright © 1961 by the President and Fellows of Harvard College. Reprinted by permission.

CONTENTS

FROM PHILO
TO SPINOZA

INTRODUCTION

Harry Austryn Wolfson (1887-1974), Nathan Littauer Professor of Hebrew Literature and Philosophy at Harvard until his retirement in 1958, was one of this century's great humanists, an erudite, versatile, and creative scholar in the history of philosophy. This little volume will, it is hoped, provide a brief, integrated overview of his significance for philosophic scholarship, a significance which may be described in the Biblical phrase as a "threefold cord which is not readily broken."

1

There is, first of all, Wolfson's impressive and rather unusual literary productivity—the justly celebrated volumes that reflect the pertinacity and profundity of his life's work: *Crescas' Critique of Aristotle: Problems of Aristotle's Physics in Jewish and Arabic Philosophy* (1929); *The Philosophy of Spinoza: Unfolding the Latent Processes of His Reasoning*, 2 vols. (1934); *Philo: Foundations of Religious Philosophy in Judaism, Christianity, and Islam*, 2 vols. (1947); *The Philosophy of the Church Fathers* (1956); *The Philosophy of Kalam* (1976); and *Kalam Repercussions in Jewish Philosophy* (in press). There are, in addition, three collections of papers and articles, some of which are full-fledged monographs of quality and scope: *Religious Philosophy: A Group of Essays* (1961); *Studies in the History of Philosophy and Religion*, vol. I (1973), vol. II (in press, 1977). Any one of these large tomes, in its own right, could and would be a scholar's pride; each would amply justify a lifetime, devoted exclusively to Hellenistic, or to patristic, or to Islamic, or to scholastic, or to Jewish sources. Indeed, Wolfson was widely acclaimed as a leading scholar in classical and medieval studies, in Judaica and Islamica, in patristics and in the humanities in general. His prodigious achievement is now a pivot of twentieth-century philosophic scholarship.

A review of Wolfson's work rivets attention on one overriding feature—its monumentality. There is a heroic dimension to the scope and substance of his achievement, which rests not only on solid learning but on intellectual daring, resourcefulness, and imaginativeness. Starting as a student of medieval Jewish philosophy (his first published article, growing out of an undergraduate paper written at Harvard, was "Maimonides and HaLevi: A Study in Typical Jewish Attitudes Toward Greek Philosophy in the Middle Ages"), Wolfson proceeded to burst the recognized bounds of specialized, sometimes provincial, scholarship, and then, patiently but vigorously, to bring within his purview the entire history of philosophy, moving with verve, aplomb, and delicacy from pre-Socratics to neo-Kantians, from Greek atomists to American pragmatists. He was fascinated and stimulated by the challenge of understanding and unraveling the origin, structure, and diversity of philosophic systems; his sustained reponse to this challenge—simultaneously erudite and imaginative—produced the pageantry and vitality of his wide-ranging scholarship.

2

The second component of this philosophic achievement—its methodological foundation—is a mode of minute textual study which Wolfson labeled the "hypothetico-deductive method," or the method of conjecture and verification, which was in essence the traditional method of studying Talmudic texts. It was, in other words, a Talmudic method of study transformed in his hands into a sharp and innovative but also controversial tool of historical-philosophical research. In the course of a long, prolific career marked by intellectual dynamism and unrelenting scholarly investigation, he was led to periodic reformulation and defense of his method. In his first major work, *Crescas' Critique of Aristotle*, the method was elegantly described:

The critical part of Crescas' works offers difficulties to the modern reader on account of its adherence to what may be called the Talmudic method of text study. In this method the starting point is the principle that any text that is deemed worthy of serious study must be assumed to have been written with such care and precision that every term, expression, generalization or exception is significant not so much for what it states as for what it implies. The contents of ideas as well as the diction and phraseology in which they are clothed are to enter into the reasoning. This method is characteristic of the Tannaitic interpretation of the Bible from the earliest times; the belief in the divine origin of the Bible was sufficient justification for attaching importance to its external forms of expression. The same method was followed later by the Amoraim in their interpretation of the Mishnah and by their successors in the interpretation of the Talmud, and it continued to be applied to the later forms of rabbinic literature. Serious students themselves, accustomed to a rigid form of logical reasoning and to the usage of precise forms of expression, the Talmudic-trained scholars attributed the same quality of precision and exactness to any authoritative work, be it of divine origin or the product of the human mind. Their attitude toward the written word of any kind is like that of the jurist toward the external phrasing of statutes and laws, and perhaps also, in some respect, like that of the latest kind of historical and literary criticism which applies the method of psychoanalysis to the study of texts.

This attitude toward texts had its necessary concomitant in what may again be called the Talmudic hypothetico-deductive method of text interpretation. Confronted with a statement on any subject, the Talmudic student will proceed to raise a series of questions before he satisfies himself of having understood its full meaning. If the statement is not clear enough, he will ask, "What does the author intend to say here?" If it is too obvious, he will again ask, "It is too plain, why then expressly say it?" If it is a statement of fact or of a concrete instance, he will then ask, "What underlying principle does it involve?" If it is a broad generalization, he will want to know exactly how much it is to include; and if it is an exception to a general rule, he will want to know how much it is to exclude. He will furthermore want to know all the circumstances under which a certain statement is true, and what qualifications are permissible. Statements apparently contradictory to each other will be reconciled by the discovery of some subtle distinction, and statements apparently irrelevant to each other will be subtly analyzed into their ultimate elements and shown to contain some common underlying principle. The harmonization of apparent contradictions and the interlinking of apparent irrelevancies are two characteristic features of the Talmudic method of text study. And similarly every other phenomenon about the text becomes a matter of investigation. Why does the author use one word rather than another? What need was there for the mentioning of a specific instance as an illustration? Do certain authorities differ or not? If they do, why do they differ? All these are legitimate questions for the Talmudic student of texts. And any attempt to answer these questions calls for ingenuity and skill, the power of analysis and association, and the ability to set up hypotheses—and all these must be bolstered by a wealth of accurate information and the use of good judgment. No limitation is set upon any subject; problems run into one another; they become intricate and interwoven, one throwing light upon the other. And there is a logic underlying this method of reasoning. It is the very same kind of logic which underlies any sort of scientific research, and by which one is enabled to form hypotheses, to test them and to formulate general laws. The Talmudic student approaches the study of texts in the same manner as the scientist approaches the study of nature. Just as the scientist proceeds on the assumption that there is a uniformity and continuity in nature so the Talmudic student proceeds on the assumption that there is a uniformity and continuity in human reasoning. Now, this method of text interpretation is sometimes derogatorily referred to as Talmudic quibbling, *pilpul*. In truth it is nothing but the application of the scientific method to the study of texts.

The same method was applied by Wolfson to the study of Spinoza's *Ethics*, in an attempt to unfold "the latent processes of his reasoning." In *The Philosophy of Spinoza*, Wolfson declared that only a scholar comfortable with Talmudic literature and trained in rabbinic methodology would be in a position to penetrate the surface of the *Ethics* and arrive at an interpretation, "historically substantiated, that will help to explain the entire *Ethics* as a logically, orderly, coherently, and intelligibly written book."

In its concentrated form of exposition and in the baffling allusiveness and ellipticalness of its style, the *Ethics* may be compared to the Talmudic and rabbinic writings upon which Spinoza was brought up, and it is in that spirit in which the old rabbinic scholars approach the study of their standard texts that we must approach the study of the *Ethics*. We must assume that the *Ethics* is a carefully written book, in which there is order and sequence and continuity, and in which every term and expression is chosen with care and used with precision. We must try to find out not only what is within it, but also what is behind it. We must try to understand not only what the author says, but also what he omits to say, and why he omits it. We must constantly ask ourselves, with regard to every statement he makes, what is the reason? What does he intend to let us hear? What is his authority? Does he reproduce his authority correctly or not? If not, why does he depart from it? What are the differences between certain statements, and can such differences be reduced to other differences, so as to discover in them a common underlying principle? In order to understand Spinoza in full and to understand him well, we must familiarize ourselves with his entire literary background. We must place ourselves in the position of students, who, having done the reading assigned in advance, come to sit at his feet and listen to his comments thereon. Every nod and wink and allusion of his will then become intelligible. Words previously quite unimportant will become charged with meaning. Abrupt transitions will receive an adequate explanation; repetitions will be accounted for. We shall know more of Spinoza's thought than what is merely expressed in his utterances. We shall know what he wished to say and what he would have said had we been able to question him and elicit further information.

His last work, on the Kalam (early medieval philosophy of Islam), published posthumously, has the following brief characterization of his method:

What is really necessary . . . is first to trace all the suggestions of foreign influence in the problems dealt with by the Mutakallimun [philosophers of Kalam] to all the possible sources available either directly to themselves or to those who may have been their oral informants; then, by the use of what may be called the hypothetico-deductive method of text interpretation, or more simply the method of conjecture and verification, which I have described elsewhere, to try to establish the origin and structure and diversity of the problems dealt with in the Kalam. Briefly stated, this method of text interpretation is analogous to what in science is called control-experiment. Just as the scientist starts out on some experiment, say, with a certain number of rabbits, so in our investigation of any topic we start out with a certain number of representative texts bearing upon that topic. Then just as the scientific experimenter inoculates only one or some of his rabbits and uses the others as controls, so we also perform all our conjectural interpretations on one or some of our texts and use the others as controls.

In all his writings, Wolfson applied this method purely and consistently, in a manner free of sociological generalizations, metahistorical hypotheses, or other popular forms of conjecture. He was particularly wary of sociological explanations which often claimed to supplant rather than to supplement historical-philological analysis and ended as smoke screens for a scholar's lack of precision. Wolfson's conjectures about a text were philological; he always tried to verify them by adducing textual evidence; he developed an interpretation and then proceeded to anchor it textually; he traced abstract problems through their terminological footprints, guided all along by his own conception of the history of philosophy. He emphasized the "earthly basis" of the history of philosophy—language and text—rather than economics, or politics, or psychology; there was constant interplay in his work between the a priori-conceptual and the empirical-textual. He had ideas which he hoped the texts would sustain.

Wolfson's critics sometimes found him to be too speculative in his unfolding of latent processes of philosophic reasoning, ready to build upon soaring conjecture without sufficient, self-evident textual verification. (His lucid expositions of complex problems and ingenious interpretations of intractable texts are punctuated by such phrases as, "it may be reasonably assumed"; "from all this we may gather"; "this explanation may be taken to reflect . . ."; etc.). He could only retort that the alternative was to be deadly, stultifying, or prosaic. It is, indeed, precisely the daring of his method which contributes both to the solidity and to the vulnerability of his achievement. The following conclusion of an article—a rejoinder to some critical comments on his explication of "four Arabic terms"—is typical: "But all this is based, of course, only upon circumstantial evidence; we have no direct testimony of [the philosophers in question] that this is exactly how their minds worked; bread-and-butter scholarship may, therefore, brush it all aside and dismiss it as unconvincing." His own erudition and ingenuity (rich, but not extravagant) prevented him from being prosaic or timid.*

It should also be noted that he was very conservative when it came to willful emendations of the text. Like sociological explanations, these, too, in his opinion, were often a defense mechanism against a scholar's failure to understand a challenging passage. Rather, he held that one should confront a textual crux squarely and exhaust all interpretative possibilities before pronouncing it corrupt or reconstructing it in one's own image. It was important to see the arbitrariness—even the whimsicality—of emendations. He applied the same caveat to the method of resolving apparent contradictions by marshaling evidence for "the

*The following declaration from *Religious Philosophy* is revealing: "Here I am going to suggest an answer for which there is no direct documentary evidence. There is only circumstantial evidence, the kind of evidence on which a defendant standing trial for muder may be acquitted by a jury of his peers, and on which, I believe, a student of the history of philosophy may venture to build a theory even at the risk of being condemned by fellow historians as indulging in flights of fancy."

interpolative character of passages" or by deciding that later editors, supposedly totally unaware of glaring contradictions, joined incongruous passages or antithetical formulations. To assume of a text that it is a mindless scissors-and-paste operation, whether by the original author or by his disciples-editors, was worthy neither of a serious scholar nor of the subject he studied. Again, the first avenue to be followed was that of conceptual interpretation. Only when this led to a dead end might the scholar resort to other methods and other solutions.

Wolfson insisted that his method, the traditional Talmudic method of text study, was identical with scientific method. In answer to a critic of his work on Crescas, Wolfson repeated emphatically:

Now, I do not feel that I have to apologize for my describing the subtleties of reasoning displayed by Crescas in handling philosophic texts as a manifestation in the field of philosophy of the traditional native Jewish method of studying texts which is generally associated with Talmudic literature. Nor do I feel the need of apologizing for the statement that in attempting to retrace the processes of Crescas' reasoning I have consciously followed this old method of Jewish learning, though externally I have tried to conform to all the accepted canons of modern scholarship. But realizing the prevalent misconceptions about this native method of Jewish learning I felt it my duty to show by an analysis of it that it is essentially a scientific method of text-study. That I have succeeded in my attempt to rehabilitate this misunderstood Talmudic method is quite evident from the reviewer's complaint that he finds no difference between it and the method followed in the best type of scholarly research.

Wolfson was regularly concerned with the advances and reverses of modern scholarship; his writings instruct us about the dangers of being uncritically overcome by fashionable "schools" and of succumbing to the use of flashy academic jargon. The frequently misunderstood traditional method which he rehabilitated—a method conducive to independence and agility of mind—may serve as a corrective to other methods which initially provide an important impetus but then lose their vigor because they are either mechanized or exaggerated.

3

Underlying this massive productivity and this meticulous analysis of so many difficult texts was a special conception of the history of philosophy which gave direction and coherence as well as resilience and originality to all of Wolfson's work. Wolfson propounded a new, anti-Hegelian scheme for the periodization of the history of philosophy— a scheme in which Jewish philosophy from Philo to Spinoza took a central place—and he expounded a philosophy of the history of philosophy in which religious thought played a major role. These twin theses are reflected in the subtitle of his study of Philo: "Foundations of Religious Philosophy in Judaism, Christianity, and Islam."

Wolfson depicts Philo as the founder of a new philosophic trend which was comtinued not only by his immediate chronological successors, the Church Fathers, but also by his indirect disciples, the Muslim, Jewish, and Christian medieval philosophers until the time of Spinoza. The distinctive and innovative feature of Philonic teachings—this feature was to be a dominant influence, latent or visible, indirect or direct, in European philosophic thought for seventeen centuries—is a well-integrated interpretation of Scripture in terms of philosophy and a balanced critique (and radical revision) of philosophy in light of Scriptural principles of belief. The Philonic system introduces philosophy into religion but simultaneously establishes the ancillary relation of philosophy to religion. Philosophy is no longer, as it was for the Greeks, a sovereign autocrat.

It is this new, historically influential type of religious philosophy which was started by Philo and abolished by Spinoza, and which is so sympathetically and imaginatively reconstructed by Wolfson. Religious principles, rooted in Scripture, lead the philosopher to restrain, reconstruct, or repudiate certain principles of classical and Greek philosophy, and this religious reconstruction of pagan philosophy is profound and far-reaching, encompassing all of medieval thought. Medieval philosophy is defined by Wolfson as "that system of thought which flourished between pagan Greek philosophy, which knew not of Scripture, and that body of philosophic writings which ever since the seventeenth century has tried to free itself from the influence of Scripture."

Medieval or religious philosophy is not for Wolfson an arid, uninspired phase bridging the ancient and modern periods but an intrinsically significant and creative philosophic adventure. There is nothing pejorative or demeaning in the term "medieval." It is not only transitional or preparatory; it is independently worthwhile, lively and aggressive, incisive, challenging, and abidingly influential.

In Wolfson's scheme Philo is presented as a daring philosopher who also introduces a major novelty in the history of philosophy—the harmonization of Scripture and philosophy. Spinoza, on the other hand, whose achievement is the cornerstone of modern philosophy, is seen not as an innovator but as a restorer. Spinoza is cast as a daring philosopher, "but he introduces no novelty. His daring consists in overthrowing the old Philonic principles which by his time had dominated the thought of European religious philosophy for some sixteen centuries." He accomplished this not by formulating new philosophical concepts or calling attention to newly discovered facts but by reviving the pre-Philonic principles of ancient Greek thought. Wolfson attempted to demonstrate that the axioms and definitions of Spinoza's *Ethics*, which were assumed to be new, are summaries of medieval views, while his reasonings are arguments against these from which he returned to pre-medieval, pagan views.*

This central conception concerning the history of philosophy—which positioned Philo, the first-century Jew of Alexandria, and Spinoza, the seventeenth-century Jew of Amsterdam, as the pivots of "medieval" philosophy—was very dear to Wolfson; it was, in many respects, the core and catalyst of his life's work. His conception of the major trends and traits of the history of philosophy—and of the epoch-making role of religious beliefs and concepts in that history—guided Wolfson in his conjectural interpretations of obscure or fragmentary passages and provided him with a reliable compass for his reconstructions of clouded philosophic positions. By identifying fixed types and standard postures, it was easier to fill in lacunae, decode elliptical texts, or flesh out sparsely formulated attitudes. His quest for unsolved problems, unexplored sources, and unperceived relationships in philosophy was nurtured to a great extent by his morphology of religious philosophy, by his delineation of the main features of Philonic thought, and by his definition of the issues involved in the confrontation of philosophy and religion. Without announcing it ceremoniously, his writing contained a full phenomenology.**

---

*Inasmuch as Wolfson's *Spinoza* was published prior to his volumes on medieval philosophy, his thesis of the medieval background was not so fully documented as would have been the case had *Spinoza* followed the volumes on Philo and medieval philosophy. Wolfson had collected much material with the idea of expanding and revising *Spinoza*, and a new edition, in three volumes, was one of his fond, but unfulfilled, hopes.

**A comparison of his treatment and structuring of the problem of faith and reason in medieval philosophy with that of Etienne Gilson (*Reason and Revelation in the Middle Ages*) and A.J. Arberry (*Revelation and Reason in Islam*) demonstrates the special qualities of his conceptualization.

Wolfson's scheme of periodization and conceptualization—developed as an explicit rebuttal of Hegel's Christianizing perception and periodication of the history of philosophy and religion—has repercussions not only for the historical study of philosophy but for its systematic study as well. Wolfson's scheme provides a perspective for approaching the problems of tradition and modernity, faith and enlightenment, and the continuities and discontinuities of history, and for assessing such related phenomena as secularism, progress, atheism, and belief, or such specific questions as revelation, free will and determinism, the nature of the soul, and immortality.

Wolfson illustrates the relevance of this perspective when, for example, he concludes his article on "The Philonic God of Revelation and His Latter-Day Deniers" with the following evaluation: "The speculation about God in modern philosophy, ever since the seventeenth century, is still a process of putting old wine into new bottles. There is only the following difference: the wine is no longer of the old vintage of the revelational theology of Scripture; it is of the old vintage of the natural or verbal theology of Greek philosophy." There is here a typology which can take religion, even in the modern era, off the defensive, for modernity itself is strikingly redefined by Wolfson as a variety of atavism or regression or archaization. In Wolfson's perspective not only Spinoza but Hume and John Stuart Mill, Leibniz and Locke, Kant and William James are seen in different contexts and in a new light. And Wolfson's scheme also provides a vantage point for characterizing and critically appraising modern expositions of Judaism—most of which he looked upon as manifestations of what Hegel would call the "disintegrated consciousness." All these reverberations of the scheme remain useful and stimulating even if some of Wolfson's conjectures are found lacking in sufficient verification or if reservations arise about the details of his interpretation of Philo or Spinoza per se.

4

A traditional method of minute textual-philological study, together with an original periodization of the history of philosophy, endows a scholar with a capacity for benign but trenchant criticism, enables him to question accepted positions and to reject the bland restatement of comfortable but unconfirmed propositions. By its nature academic scholarship tends to become institutionalized and to develop its own orthodoxies, pieties, and platitudes; this is perhaps especially true of scholarship that prides itself on being modern and up-to-date. In the face of such entrenched views a traditional perspective, finely honed and controlled with historical insight, can hurl a challenge and release bracing currents of fresh air. The scholar holding this perspective may assume the necessary role of the gadfly, and show how the tyranny of the present is potentially worse than the tyranny of the past.

The two essays reprinted here, from *Philo* and from *Religious Philosophy*, show beautifully and forcefully how—given Wolfson's method—Philo erected the new type of philosophy and Spinoza pulled it down. As far as Wolfson's own achievement is concerned, "the rest is commentary. . . ."

WHAT IS NEW IN PHILO?

WHAT IS NEW IN PHILO?

WE ALL have a feeling that between ancient Greek philosophy which knew not Scripture and the philosophy which ever since the seventeenth century has tried to free itself from the influence of Scripture there was a philosophy which placed itself at the service of Scripture and was willing to take orders from it. As to what this intervening period in the history of philosophy should be called, historians offer us two choices. Sometimes they call it "Mediaeval Philosophy" and start it with the Church Fathers in the second century,[1] even though in political history the mediaeval period is generally supposed to start many centuries later, either with the death of Theodosius in 395 or with the fall of Rome in 476. Sometimes, however, they call it "Christian Philosophy"[2] and reserve the term mediaeval as a description of that part of Christian philosophy which begins with St. Augustine (354–430) or with Boethius (480–524),[3] both of whom lived close enough respectively to the dates which are generally considered as the beginning of the mediaeval period politically.

But scholarship likes to adorn itself with footnotes and to garnish itself with appendixes. And so the main text of the history of philosophy is generally annotated by, or has appended to it, two philosophical incidents. The first of these incidents is the philosophy of Philo, which is introduced

[1]Cf. J.H. Erdmann, *A History of Philosophy*, I, 225 ff.
[2]Cf. Ueberweg-B. Geyer, *Die patristische und scholastische Philosophie* (1928), pp. 1, 3, and 141; E. Gilson and Ph. Böhmer, *Die Geschichte der christlichen Philosophie* (1937).
[3]Cf. M. De Wulf, *History of Mediaeval Philosophy*,[3] I, 1-23; 77-82; 105-114.

·as a postscript to ancient Greek philosophy. The second incident is Arabic Moslem and Jewish philosophy, which is introduced as a prefatory note to the scholasticism of the thirteenth century. The value of these two philosophic incidents, it must be admitted, is not entirely overlooked; in their subordinate position they are dutifully evaluated; but whatever value is attached to them is that of furnishing certain ingredients in the reconstruction of the background of two periods in Christian philosophy — in the case of the former that of the Church Fathers and in the case of the latter that of the scholasticism of the thirteenth century.

On the whole, this treatment of the history of philosophy reflects that prevailing conception of history in general which, as theologically formulated by Eusebius and St. Augustine, maintains that everything that came before Christianity is to be considered only as preparatory to it and everything that happened outside of Christianity is to be considered only as tributary to it. In Hegel's metaphysical restatement of this theological conception of history, the particular application of this view to the history of philosophy is bluntly stated without any circumlocution. "The history of philosophy," he says, "falls into three periods — that of Greek philosophy, the philosophy of the Middle Ages and modern philosophy," [4] the first of which "has found its place in the religion of the heathen," whereas the second and third have their sphere "within the Christian world," [5] for the philosophy of the Middle Ages, in which the scholastics are to be included, "mainly falls within the Christian Church," [6] and similarly modern philosophy, which is essentially "Teutonic philosophy," is also "philosophy within Christendom." [7] Though "Arabians and Jews

[4]Hegel, *History of Philosophy*, I, 109.   [6]*Ibid.*, I, 110.
[5]*Ibid.*, III, 1; cf. I, 101.   [7]*Ibid.*, I, 101.

are also historically to be noticed," [8] they "have only to be noticed in an external and historic way." [9] As for Philo, he says, "we must make cursory mention of" him, before we enter upon our discussion of "the Neo-Platonists," [10] the latter of which are to be considered as being "closely connected with the revolution which was caused in the world by Christianity" [11] though only as a sort of precursor to its philosophy, for, as he adds, while the Neo-Platonists had some adumbration of "the Idea of Christianity," [12] they "still had not proved their doctrine that the Trinity is the truth." [13]

There is much to be said on this conception of the history of philosophy, both for it and against it. One could go on and argue endlessly whether historical facts, and facts in the history of philosophy in particular, are to be studied — to use the language of Aristotle — as *known to us* or as *known by nature*, and consequently one could also go on and argue endlessly whether in our attempt to break up the continuity of historical events into periods we should look at all for any differentiating characteristics other than those which are visibly known to us and which have palpably proved themselves of consequence in the experience of a great part of mankind who share common beliefs and a common way of life. But such speculative arguments would lead us nowhere. They would be as useless as the old-fashioned speculations as to how to classify species, when species were held to be unalterably and firmly fixed from creation and their classifications were only half-intuitive generalizations based upon inadequate data superficially studied. When, however, as a result of a century's research, beginning with Linnaeus and ending in Darwin's voyage on H. M. S. Beagle, investigators began to base their speculations concerning

---

[8] *Ibid.*, I, 110. [10] *Ibid.*, II, 387. [12] *Ibid.*, III, 1.
[9] *Ibid.*, III, 1. [11] *Ibid.*, I, 374. [13] *Ibid.*, III, 2.

species on extensive accumulations of specimens and the study of the internal structures of those specimens, the various attempts at their classification from then on were based upon a solid foundation of reality, even though the boundary lines between species were no longer firmly fixed. Let us also set sail on some Beagle of our own in search of philosophic specimens and, after we have found them, let us study their internal structures and then, from their internal structures, let us try to learn something about the origin and classification of their species, which species we commonly call periods in the history of philosophy or systems of philosophy. It is also possible that as a result of such an investigation so-called periods and systems of philosophy might prove to be not so distinctly and deeply separated from each other as they are generally assumed to be.

The specimens which we bring back from the voyage on our own Beagle are in the form of books, printed books and manuscript books, books preserved in their entirety and books of which only fragments have been preserved in other books, and books of which only the titles have been preserved. In our study of our specimens, we begin, as every scientific study of a subject usually begins, with a classification of them. Taking first as the basis of our classification that which externally differentiates them from one another, namely, language, we find that they fall into five groups, Greek, Latin, Syriac, Arabic, and Hebrew. The Greek specimens date from the fragments of pre-Socratic philosophers to the fifteenth century, falling short by about a century of the reputed end of mediaeval philosophy. The Latin specimens date from Cicero and continue to the end of mediaeval philosophy. The Syriac specimens, the smallest of the five groups, date from the fifth to about the end of the thirteenth century. The Arabic specimens date from the eighth to the end of the twelfth century. The Hebrew specimens date from the tenth century and continue to the reputed end of the medieval period of philosophy.

Continuing then to examine the contents of these specimens, we discover that these five linguistic groups are not independent of each other. To begin with, the last four of them are all dependent upon the Greek specimens. In all of them Greek works are translated, names of Greek philosophers are quoted, certain Greek terms are transliterated in their own respective alphabets, many more Greek terms are translated literally in their own respective languages, and problems of Greek philosophy invariably form the starting point of discussions. Then, the last four of these five groups have certain relations among themselves. Some philosophic specimens are translated from the Syriac into Arabic or are Syriac paraphrases of Arabic works; Some are translated from the Arabic into Hebrew and a few from Hebrew into Arabic; some are translated from both Arabic and Hebrew into Latin; some are translated from the Latin into Hebrew; and together with these translations there go also the adoption of terminology, both in transliterated and translated forms, the quotation of names, and the borrowing of ideas.

Studying our philosophic specimens still more closely, we notice that all of them are streaked through with material drawn from another type of literature, namely, the religious literature. But with respect to this streak of religious literature which runs through the entire field of philosophy, we notice that not long before the rise of Christianity a sudden change takes place in the type of literature drawn upon. Before that time in Greek and also Latin philosophy, and for some time after that in a certain part of Greek and Latin philosophy, the religious literature drawn upon, in the form of quotations, references, or allusions, is pagan Greek literature. But beginning with that time the religious literature drawn upon is that of Scripture in its threefold division, the so-called Old and New Testaments and the Koran. This scriptural streak in its threefold division is variously distributed in our five groups of philosophic specimens. In the Greek philosophic specimens, those dating from before the middle of the first century of the Christian era are Jewish and quote the Old Testament, but those dating after that period are all Christian and quote both the Old and the New Testament. The Latin specimens, beginning with Tertullian toward the end of the second century, are all Christian, and the quotations are from both the Old and the New Testament. The Syriac specimens are Christian, and the quotations in them are from both the Old and the New Testament. The Arabic specimens are both Moslem and Jewish and to a lesser extent also Christian. The Moslems quote only the Koran, the Jews only the Old Testament, and the Christians both the Old and the New Testament. The Hebrew specimens are only Jewish and the Scripture quoted is only the Old Testament. Not only, however, is this break from ancient pagan philosophy marked by a change in the quotations from religious literature, but it is also marked by a new form of philosophic literary expression. Before that time the forms of philosophic literary expression were the gnomic saying, the dialogue, the poem, the diatribe, and the formal discourse. From now on a new form of exposition appears in philosophic literature, the homily on some scriptural text or the running commentary upon some scriptural books.

This change in the type of religious literature drawn upon and in literary form, we discover upon still further study, is not a mere matter of externality; it marks a fundamental break in philosophic doctrines, which break ushers in a fundamentally new period in the history of philosophy, that intermediate or mediaeval period which we all feel intervenes between ancient philosophy which knew not Scripture and modern philosophy which began with an attempt to free itself from Scripture. Mediaeval philosophy, so defined and delimited, is thus the common philosophy of three religions — Judaism, Christianity, and Islam — consisting of one philosophy written in five languages — Greek, Latin, Syriac, Arabic, and Hebrew. It is indeed a continuation of pagan Greek philosophy but at the same time also a radical revision of that philosophy, stressing certain doctrines by which it is distinguished from ancient pagan philosophy. From its very beginning in its original language, even before its spread into other languages, it formed a new school of Greek philosophy, more distinct in fundamental problems from the totality of all the pagan Greek schools of philosophy than those pagan schools are distinct from one another. When we speak of Christian philosophy, and for that matter also of Jewish or Moslem philosophy, and the question is raised as to what we mean thereby apart from Greek philosophic problems dealt with by Christians or Jews or Moslems, or apart from the employment of certain concepts or a certain form of reasoning from Greek philosophy in defense of certain religious doctrines borrowed from Scripture,[14] the answer to be given is that it is a fundamental revision of Greek philosophy on the basis of certain principles common to these three religions, resulting in the introduction of new elements into every branch of pagan Greek philosophy — its epistemology, its metaphysics, its physics, and its ethics.

Let us then take a fleeting glance at these common principles which constitute the common characteristics of that

---

[14]See the collection of forty-seven opinions as to the meaning of Christian philosophy in E. Gilson, *L'Esprit de la Philosophie Médiévale* (1932), I, 297-324, and Gilson's own discussion on the subject in chs. i and ii.

mediaeval philosophy and let us invent a synthetic mediaeval philosopher, made up of all the common elements of the Christian, the Moslem, and the Jewish philosopher, and let us follow in the track of his reasoning as he proceeds to revise Greek philosophy.

Our synthetic mediaeval philosopher begins with the belief that there is one infallible source of truth, and that is revelation, and that revelation is embodied in Scripture, be it Old Testament or New Testament or Koran. In Scripture he finds a description of the world, perhaps not so full as he would have liked to have, but he finds in it enough references to water and earth and air and fire and heavens and stars and minerals and plants and living beings to furnish him with enough materials for an orderly description of the world as he knows it. He also finds in it an explanation of those things which he wants to know about the world, how it came into being and how it is governed. Finally, he finds in it rules for the guidance of man in his various relations to his fellow men, both as an individual to other individuals and as a member of society to the society of which he is a part.

But the God who furnished certain men with certain truths directly by revelation has also equipped men with reason. Thus equipped, certain men were able by their own effort to discover some of those truths which God made known to other men directly by revelation — to discover the nature of the world, to describe it, to explain it, and to lay down rules for the conduct of mankind. And just as the truths of revelation are embodied in the threefold Scripture, written in Hebrew, Greek, and Arabic, so the truths discovered by reason are embodied in a philosophic literature written primarily in Greek. Two bodies of literature thus contain all human wisdom: one the wisdom made known through revelation; the other the wisdom discovered by reason.

Since God is the author both of the truths made known by revelation and of the truths discovered by reason, there can be no conflict between them. If a conflict should appear to exist between them, it must be no real conflict. Any such conflict must be due either to our misunderstanding of Scripture or to the vagaries of human reason which has gone astray. For revelation must of necessity be communicated to man in the language commonly spoken by man, and such a language does not always convey to the ordinary man the real meaning intended by the revelation. Similarly, human reason must of necessity be encased in a human body and function through a human body, and thus, hemmed in by a body, reason sometimes is led astray and errs. Scripture, to our synthetic mediaeval philosopher, is always true, if only its language could be properly understood; reason would always be true, if only it were not misguided by the body in which it is encased. In the proper study of the relation of Scripture to reason, therefore, Scripture has to be interpreted in the light of what is most evidently true in reason, and reason has to be corrected in the light of what is most evidently the true teachings of Scripture. There may be differences of opinion, among those who make up our synthetic philosopher, as to what is most evidently true in reason as well as to what is most obviously the true teaching of Scripture, but they all agree that this is the proper method of procedure.[15]

And so our synthetic philosopher begins to compare the teachings of Scripture with the teachings of philosophy.

Among the teachings of Scripture our synthetic philosopher finds principles which he assumes to constitute what

[15]H.A. Wolfson, *Philo*, I, 155-163, 194-199.

Scripture considers as essential to any true religion, namely, the existence of God, the unity of God, creation of the world, divine providence, and the divine origin of the rules for human conduct.[16] He then begins to look into the writings of the philosophers to see what reason has discovered about these principles.

He finds that with the exception of one school of philosophers, the Epicureans, reason has guided all the philosophers to the discovery of the existence of God.[17] He is delighted with the arguments advanced by reason in proof of the existence of God; he appropriates them and makes use of them. He makes a few changes in some of them, especially in the argument which maintains that the existence of God is an innate idea, but on the whole he is willing to follow the pagan philosophers in the proofs they have discovered by reason.[18]

He also finds that reason has led philosophers to discover that God is numerically one and, like Scripture, to come out against popular polytheism. Reason has also led some philosophers, like Plato and Aristotle, to discover that God is internally one, in the sense that He is incorporeal, though some philosophers, like the Stoics, have been led astray by reason to think that God is himself corporeal and never leaves the inwards of the corporeal world. Similarly, reason has led philosophers to discover that God is one in the sense of His being self-sufficient and in need of nothing outside himself,[19] though they do not exploit that property of God to its full extent.

But he finds that reason has failed to guide philosophers to the discovery of two other phases of the unity of God.

First, unlike Scripture, reason has failed to see the unity

16Cf. *ibid.*
17Cf. *ibid.*

18Cf. *ibid.*
19Cf. *ibid.*

of God as implying His uniqueness in the sense of His being the only one who is both uncreated and a creator. In Plato, God is indeed spoken of as a creator, but by the side of God there are to Plato also ideas, concerning which he sometimes says that they are uncreated and that they possess a creative power of their own. In Aristotle, God is spoken of mainly as a mover, not as a creator, and the world, which is not God, is spoken of as being uncreated. Our synthetic philosopher, in opposition to all this, does not admit by the side of God anything that possesses a creative power of its own and anything that is uncreated; and, if he is occasionally inclined to admit the existence of something coeternal with God, he will try to show that its eternity does not mean uncreatedness.[20]

Second, unlike Scripture, reason has failed to conceive of the unity and unlikeness of God as implying the unknowability and indescribability of His essence. Neither Plato nor Aristotle, despite their belief in the immateriality and simplicity and indivisibility of God, had any conception of the unknowability of God's essence and its indescribability. Indeed our synthetic philosopher will be unable to make up his mind as to what extent God is unknowable and indescribable, and in what sense one is to understand the terms by which as a rule God is described. But he starts his philosophy with a principle of the unknowability and the indescribability of God; and, while he is conscious of the difficulties that this principle may give rise to, he debates these difficulties in his own mind and finds some kind of solution for them without giving up that principle.[21]

Less satisfactory to our synthetic philosopher and requiring correction by him is the finding of reason with regard to the problem of the origin of the world. While reason has

[20]Cf. *ibid.*   [21]Cf. *ibid.*

led some philosophers to regard our present world as having been created out of some preëxistent matter, it has led others to regard it as eternal. For himself, our synthetic philosopher is unable to make up his mind as to the real meaning of the teaching of Scripture with regard to the beginning of the world, though he is inclined to favor the view, never envisaged by reason, that the world came into being *ex nihilo.* But of one thing he is certain: however the world came into being, its coming into being must be so conceived as to make God the cause of its being. Of one other thing is he certain: however the world came into being, it came into being by the will of God, which will of God is to be understood in such a way as to lead to the conclusion that had God willed it He could have created a different kind of world.[22]

Still less satisfactory to our synthetic philosopher and requiring correction by him is the finding of reason with regard to divine providence. On the whole, reason has led philosophers to believe that the world is governed by certain laws, laws which make for order and stability, for permanence and preservation, as if some wise being were presiding over it and supervising it and caring for it. Philosophers even speak of the laws of nature as being the work of God. In Plato they are said to be implanted in the world by the Demiurge at the time of His creation of the world. In Aristotle they are said to be the immutable movements imparted to the world by the prime mover who is God. In the Stoics they are said to be the working of the primordial fire, out of which the world unfolded itself but which continues to abide in the world as an internal Reason. The philosophers also sometimes describe these laws of nature as divine

22Cf. *ibid.*

providence. But their divine providence is fated; more often and more correctly do they describe it by the term fate. The laws of nature which they trace to their respective gods are absolutely unchangeable, inexorable; even their gods cannot change them. There is no room in their systems for miracles and individual providence.

Now our synthetic philosopher, on the whole, agrees with the finding of reason that there are immutable laws of nature. God to him is not only the creator of the world but also the cause of its preservation and its governance and its orderly processes. God it is who has implanted in the world that order and regularity of the recurrence of events which we call laws of nature. Because God is unchangeable, these laws of nature which He has implanted in the world are also unchangeable. Still, with all their unchangeability, God has reserved to himself the right of a free agent to change these laws of His own making. The possibility of miracles is a fundamental belief which our synthetic philosopher will insist upon. He may offer different explanations of miracles; he may not be quite certain what extraordinary events reported in the various religious Scriptures and traditions are to be regarded as miracles; but he does not question the principle that God is a free agent who can change the order of nature and perform miracles. This principle is the basis of our synthetic philosopher's belief that divine providence is individual. To him, God's implanting of laws of nature in the universe is a token of His universal providence, for these laws of nature are for the purpose of the preservation of the world as a whole and of all the kinds of genera and species within it. But the upsetting of these laws of nature by God through the working of miracles is to our synthetic philosopher a token of God's individual providence, for these miracles have for their purpose the preservation of

individuals or groups of individuals when all the forces of
nature are lined up against them for their destruction.[23]

As a corollary to the conception of freedom in God is the
conception of freedom in man, and on this point, too, our
synthetic philosopher finds that reason has gone astray and
failed to attain to the truth of the matter. Man, say the
philosophers, is a part of nature, and as everything in nature
is determined so also everything in human nature is determined. There is no such thing as freedom, by which man
can break the chain of causes which have led him up to the
point of being faced with the making of a decision. If Plato
and Aristotle and the Stoics do speak of a distinction in
human actions between actions which are voluntary and
actions which are compulsory, they mean by voluntary
actions only actions that are performed without ignorance
and without external compulsion. To the philosophers, all
the forces that bear upon human action are divided into
forces of emotion and forces of reason. When man is faced
with a choice between two alternative modes of action, the
choice, according to them, will be determined, as in the case
of any physical conflict in nature between opposing forces,
by the relative strength of the forces of reason and the
forces of emotion. If the forces of reason are stronger, the
victory will be that of reason; if the forces of emotion are
stronger, the victory will be that of the emotions. Will itself is merely a description of that choice determined either
by reason or by the emotions; there is no such thing as a will
which is free and independent of these forces of reason and
emotion. If philosophers urge man to act in accordance with
the dictates of reason, it does not mean that they believe
that at the crucial moment which calls for a decision man is
free to choose whether to follow the dictates of reason or the

[23]Cf. *ibid.*

dictates of the emotions. It is only an exhortation to man that he should continually, throughout his lifetime, cultivate and strengthen his reason, by the only means by which reason can be cultivated and strengthened, and that is by the acquisition of knowledge, so that when the crucial moment arrives reason will be found the stronger force and will dominate the emotions.

Our synthetic mediaeval philosopher is opposed to this. Man, indeed, may be considered as part of nature and as subject to its laws. But just as the laws of nature may be upset by God's freedom, so also the laws which govern human action, as part of nature, may be upset by man's freedom. Our synthetic philosopher is indeed conscious of the many difficulties which this belief in human freedom gives rise to and in his attempt to solve all these difficulties he may make all kinds of qualifications as to the nature and exercise of this freedom, but despite all this he will cling strenuously to the belief that the human soul is endowed by God with part of His own power of freedom, to work miracles in man as He himself works miracles in the world. When man is faced with a decision and the forces of his own nature are all set so as to determine his decision in one particular way, he can by the freedom with which he is endowed by God decide to act contrary to all those determining forces. Only external obstacles or forces can defeat the free human decision, for by these external obstacles or forces man may be prevented from acting according to his own free choice or he may be forced even to act contrary to his own free choice, but even these external obstacles and forces may be miraculously removed by God, if man is found worthy of such a direct divine intervention.[24]

Another corollary to the belief in God's freedom and hence

[24]Cf. *ibid.*

also to human freedom is the belief that the immortality of the soul depends by the will of God upon one's individual conduct, so that while each soul can be immortal it can also be destroyed. Now our synthetic philosopher is ready to admit that reason also has led some pagan philosophers, and especially Plato, to a belief in the immortality of the soul, and he may perhaps be also ready to admit that it was the teachings of pagan philosophy that led him to discover the full meaning of this principle in the pages of his Scriptures, but he will insist that reason has failed to discover the full truth of that belief. To those pagan philosophers, even when they have that belief, immortality is assumed to belong to the soul by the necessity of its very nature and hence not only may it be immortal but it must be so. Even to those pagan philosophers who happen to speak of a certain kind of destructibility of the soul, this destructibility also comes to it by a necessary process of nature; it is not the result of individual divine providence. To our synthetic philosopher, however, immortality is a special gift of God and an exercise of individual divine providence. The soul, which is assumed by him to have an existence of its own in the human body, is endowed by God not only with freedom but also with immortality, for by its own nature, like anything else created by God, it cannot be immortal. Of this gift of immortality man must prove himself worthy, and he can prove himself worthy of it only by the exercise of his freedom in a manner approved of by God. If man does not prove himself worthy of immortality, he forfeits it; his soul may suffer destruction. Our synthetic philosopher is perhaps not always quite certain as to how the soul remains immortal as an individual entity and as to how it suffers destruction. But after all his debating with himself on the problem, he comes out with a confession of a belief that each man's soul may by God's grace survive in some sense as an individual entity but of itself it is subject to some kind of destruction.[25]

Finally, a third corollary of divine freedom and hence also of human freedom is the divine origin of morality. To our synthetic mediaeval philosopher the efforts of pagan philosophers to attain by human reason perfect rules for the conduct of men, both as individuals and as members of society, have by their own confession proved to fall short of perfection. To him, the only rule of conduct which is perfect is that which has been revealed by God, for if, as the pagan philosophers maintain, perfect rules of conduct must be in accordance with nature and in accordance with reason, they cannot be discovered by reason, for reason itself never attains perfection in its knowledge of nature; they can be perfect only when revealed by God who is the creator of both reason and nature. In his study of the laws revealed by God, carefully comparing them with the teachings of the pagan philosophers, our synthetic philosopher finds in the divine laws the perfect fulfillment of all that the pagan philosophers have vainly striven to attain. Indeed our synthetic philosopher may debate with himself whether that divine law was to continue eternally to be the Law revealed to Moses, or whether the Law of Moses was to be replaced in part by the law of the Gospels and the Apostles, or whether even this latter law was to be replaced by the law of the Koran; but whatever decision he may arrive at on this particular question he remains firm in his belief that man's conduct is to be guided by a divine law.[26]

These are the main principles of our synthetic mediaeval philosopher. The endless discussions to be found in the voluminous literature of the various languages in which mediaeval philosophy is embodied are only elaborations upon

[25]Cf. *ibid.*   [26]Cf. *ibid.*

these principles — explanations of these principles in their manifold implications, discussions of various difficulties arising from these principles, homilies on various scriptural proof-texts advanced in support of them, and discourses on various philosophical passages which appear to be either in agreement or disagreement with them. Taken altogether, these principles of mediaeval philosophy constitute a radical departure from ancient pagan Greek philosophy — they radically change its theory of knowledge, by introducing into it a new source of knowledge; they radically change its metaphysics, by introducing a new conception into the nature and causality of God, who is the main subject of metaphysics; they radically change its physics, by introducing a new conception into the working of its laws; they radically change its ethics, by introducing a new source of morality. The changes thus introduced by our synthetic philosopher into Greek philosophy are as great as those introduced into it by Plato and greater than those introduced into it by any other philosopher after Plato. Our synthetic mediaeval philosopher, indeed, has not introduced anything radically new into what he learned from pagan Greek philosophic works about the description of the structure and composition of the physical universe. He was quite willing to follow Aristotle in his description of the heavens, of the earth, of growing and living things, of the human body, of the human soul, and of the rules of human reasoning, though not without an occasional grumble and not without an occasional excursus into the writings of some other Greek philosophers. He assiduously studied the works of Aristotle as well as those of other Greek philosophers dealing with these subjects, commenting upon them, paraphrasing them, epitomizing them, questioning and disputing about them, and even making some slight original contributions in the course of his study of them — but all this in harmony with those fundamental principles which set off his own philosophy from that of the Greek philosophers. Similarly, when toward the end of mediaeval philosophy, in the sixteenth century, new conceptions of nature and of the physical universe began to make their appearance, exponents of mediaeval philosophy, among whom Descartes is to be included, tried to show how easy it was for them to adjust their inherited principles of mediaeval philosophy to their new conception of nature and the physical universe.

This fundamental departure from pagan Greek philosophy, if the facts of the history of philosophy are to be presented as they are actually *known by nature* and not as they merely happen to be *known to us*, appears first in Hellenistic Judaism,[27] where it attains its systematic formulation in Philo. Philo is the founder of this new school of philosophy, and from him it directly passes on to the Gospel of St. John and the Church Fathers, from whom it passes on to Moslem and hence also to mediaeval Jewish philosophy. Philo is the direct or indirect source of this type of philosophy which continues uninterruptedly in its main assertions for well-nigh seventeen centuries, when at last it is openly challenged by Spinoza.

Historically, a certain nibbling at this type of philosophy, which is properly to be called the Philonic philosophy, started before Spinoza; and historically, too, Philonic philosophy did not completely disappear even after Spinoza. But Spinoza it was who for the first time launched a grand assault upon it, and if the Philonic philosophy did not completely disappear as a result of that assault, it no longer held a dominant position. Henceforth, in order to gain attention at all, it had to disguise its meaning and adopt a new vocabu-

[27]Cf. *ibid.*

lary. It is only recently that Philonic philosophy, through the increasing influence of one of its most distinguished Mediaeval Christian exponents, began to gain vogue and currency in quarters where it is not an inherited tradition, but that is due only to the breakdown of philosophy as a learned discipline, from which some inquiring minds try to seek escape in scholasticism as a substitute for scholarship.

In his grand assault upon Philonic philosophy, Spinoza starts with an attack upon its chief basis, the belief in revelation. This part of his assault he makes in his *Tractatus Theologico-Politicus*,[28] a work written in the Philonic manner, in the form of homilies upon scriptural texts. With his denial of revelation, he then undertakes to restore philosophy to the status in which it was prior to the Philonic revolution. Like most Greek philosophers, he does not deny the existence of God, if by God is meant what the Greek philosopher meant by the principle of causality in the world.[29] Like the Greek philosophers, he similarly does not deny the unity of God, understanding by unity not only the numerical oneness of the cause of the world but also its self-sufficiency and simplicity. Moreover, like Aristotle in the Neoplatonized form in which he understood him, he takes the unity of God to mean His uniqueness as an uncaused cause. He denies, however, with some qualification, the Philonic tradition that the simplicity of God means also His unknowability and indefinability.[30] But, in this particular instance, going beyond the Philonic tradition, he comes out even against the Platonic and Aristotelian tradition which takes the simplicity of God to mean His incorporeality.[31] Then, going back

28Cf. *ibid.*
29Cf. the present writer's *The Philosophy of Spinoza*, chapters on "Proofs of the Existence of God" and "The Causality of God."
30Cf. *Philo.*
31Cf. *ibid.*

to general classical Greek philosophy, he denies God that
supposed freedom of the will by which He can change the
order of nature, though by a special definition of the term
freedom he calls the necessity of God's action by the name
of freedom.[32] Again going back to general classical Greek
philosophy, he denies man that vaunted freedom of his
with which Philonic philosophy has endowed him as a gift
of God.[33] With Aristotle, he also denies the separability of
soul from body,[34] though by following the Neoplatonized
form of Aristotelianism he speaks of the immortality of the
soul, and even of an individual immortality, without resort-
ing to the Philonic view of the destructibility of the soul.[35]
Finally, without a belief in revelation, he goes back to the
classical tradition of Greek philosophy in restoring to
reason its paramount position as the source of morality.[36]

This, then, is the new period in the history of philosophy,
ushered in by Philo and ushered out by Spinoza. If we still
choose to describe this period as mediaeval, for after all it
comes between a philosophy which knew not of Scripture
and a philosophy which tries to free itself from Scripture,
then mediaeval philosophy is the history of the philosophy
of Philo. For well-nigh seventeen centuries this Philonic
philosophy dominated European thought. Nothing really
new happened in the history of European philosophy during that extended period. The long succession of philosophers
during that period, from among whom various figures are
selected by various historians for special distinction as in-
novators, have only tried to expound, each in his own way,

[32]Cf. *The Philosophy of Spinoza*, chapters on "The Causality of God" and "Necessity
and Purposelessness."
[33]Cf. *ibid.*, same chapters and also chapter on "Will."
[34]Cf. *Philo.*
[35]Cf. *ibid.*
[36]Cf. *ibid.*

the principles laid down by Philo. To the question, then, what is new in Philo? the answer is that it was he who built up that philosophy, just as the answer to the question what is new in Spinoza? is that it was he who pulled it down.[37]

[37]Cf. *The Philosophy of Spinoza*, chapter on "What Is New in Spinoza?"

SPINOZA AND THE RELIGION OF THE PAST

SPINOZA AND THE RELIGION OF
THE PAST *

A COMPREHENSIVE study of Spinoza's attitude toward religion would of necessity fall into three parts. For Spinoza, who is known to us primarily as a philosopher, was also a historian of religion and a political thinker. As a historian of religion, which in his time meant a student of the Bible, he had certain definite views on the development of religious ideas and institutions in both the Old and the New Testament. These views are to be found in his *Tractatus Theologico-Politicus*. As a political thinker Spinoza, like many of his contemporaries, was especially preoccupied with the problem of the relation between Church and State, concerning which he had certain definite views. These views are to be found, again, in his *Tractatus Theologico-Politicus* and also in his unfinished *Tractatus Politicus*. Finally, as a philosopher he dealt with all the abstruse and abstract problems of traditional religious philosophy. The discussion of these problems is to be found in the *Ethics*. It is with the *Ethics* that I am going to deal tonight.

The *Ethics* — as I have tried to show in *The Philosophy of Spinoza* — is primarily a criticism of fundamental principles of religious philosophy, which at the beginning of the Christian era were laid down by Philo and were still in vogue at the time of Spinoza in the seventeenth century. This criticism is constructed according to an old forensic device which may be described as "yes" and "but." The "yes" part is an expression of Spinoza's assent to the external formulation of some of the principles of traditional religious philosophy. The "but" part is a statement of the special sense in which he himself is willing to use that formulation. Between these two

*Delivered as the Horace M. Kallen Lecture at the New School for Social Research in 1949; published by the New School in 1950, and reprinted in *The Menorah Journal* (1950), 146-167.

parts is a whole chain of complicated arguments. To the general reader this structure of Spinoza's thought is not obvious, for it is obscured by the artificial form in which the *Ethics* is written — the geometrical form. It is for this reason that the *Ethics* is one of the most difficult books in philosophic literature. It is for this reason also that the *Ethics*, in my opinion, has so often been misunderstood and so often misinterpreted.

Spinoza begins from the very beginning. He asks himself, What is the most fundamental assumption underlying the religious philosophies of Judaism, Christianity, and Islam? And after examining various possibilities he settles on one. It is the belief that over and above and beyond the aggregate of things which make up this our physical universe there is something unlike the universe.

Had Spinoza written his *Ethics* after the manner of the rabbis and the scholastics he would have quoted here verses from Scripture in which men are challenged to produce something which is like unto God. As to what that unlikeness between God and the universe consisted in, Spinoza must have found a variety of opinions among religious philosophers. Most of them, and Philo at their head, following the tradition of Plato and Aristotle, interpreted that unlikeness between God and the world as meaning that, unlike the world which is material, God is immaterial. Others, of whom Tertullian is the chief example, either consciously or unconsciously following the Stoics, argued that the unlikeness between God and the world meant that, unlike the world which consists of one kind of matter, God consists of another kind of matter.

But there is one sense of unlikeness between God and the world upon which, Spinoza must have found, all religious philosophers were in agreement. They all believed that, unlike the world which is dependent upon God, God is independent of the world. This independence of God may be expressed by the term separateness — separateness in the sense that the existence of God does not necessarily imply the existence of the world. For believing, as all of them did, that the world came into existence after it had not been in existence, they also believed that prior to the existence of the world there was a God without a world. And believing, as some of them did, that some day the world will come to an end, they also believed that after the ultimate destruction of the world there will be God, again, without a world. And since God was and will be without a world, even now when the world exists, God's existence is independent of the world, separate from it, and apart from it.

To this principle Spinoza begins by saying "yes." Yes, he is willing to admit that there is something over and above and beyond the aggregate of things which constitutes this physical universe of ours. He is not an antiquated Epicurean to whom the world was a mere conglomeration of aimlessly flying indivisible particles of bodies. He is even willing to call that something by the name of God, for, as he so often says, he does not care to argue about words. But — and here his first "but" comes in — he is unwilling to admit that the something unlike the constituent parts of the universe is separate from the universe. Within the universe itself and inseparable from it, he maintains, there is something unlike its parts. And as he proceeds in his argument he explains that by that something he means the wholeness of the universe, which he contends is not the mere aggregate of its parts. In support of this contention, he alludes to two old propositions which by his time were already philosophic commonplaces. The first proposition is that the universe is an organic living being, a view which ever since Plato had been expressed by various philosophers in various ways. The second proposition is that in an organic living being the whole is something different from the mere sum of its parts.

This is a clear and simple thought which Spinoza could have expressed in clear and simple language. But being a philosopher, he felt that he owed it to his profession to express himself in technical language, even at the risk of making clear things obscure and simple things complicated. And so, rummaging through the stockpile of philosophic terminology, he came upon the term *substance*. This he pasted as a label upon that wholeness of the universe of which we have been speaking: a label used by Spinoza as the equivalent for the traditional term God.

The choice, it must be said, was not a happy one. For already by the time of Spinoza the term *substance* had a variety of conflicting meanings, and the one exclusive meaning which he now gave to it only tended to add to the confusion of those who later began to study his *Ethics*.

Then from the same stockpile Spinoza pulled out the term *mode*, which he used as a label for the particular things in the universe. And inasmuch as the particular things are many and can be classified in a variety of ways, Spinoza has a variety of *modes* variously classified.

The choice of the term *mode* as a designation for particular things was also unfortunate. For the term *mode*, historically, had already acquired the meaning of something unreal, something which is only apparent. And so its use by Spinoza led many of those who later began the study of his *Ethics* to read a false meaning into what he meant by particular things.

Finally, out of several reminiscent terms and expressions, Spinoza coined a new phrase of his own, "the face of the whole universe," which he uses as a description of the aggregate of particular things of the universe, or of the particular *modes*, which to him is to be distinguished from the wholeness of the universe.

All this is the first point in Spinoza's criticism of traditional philosophy. He then takes up another point.

To traditional philosophy, God, though independent of the universe, is still not unrelated to it. His relation to the universe, which is that of creator and preserver, is expressed by traditional philosophers in their description of God as the efficient and formal and final cause of the world. They could not exactly agree on the manner in which God created the world — whether it was after the manner of a potter who molds a vessel out of clay, or after the manner of a magician who pulls rabbits out of the emptiness of his hat. But whether God created the world out of a pre-existent matter or whether He created it out of nothing, they all insisted that He created it by will and design. For, if He willed it, He need have created no world at all. And, again, if He willed it, He could have created a different kind of world.

And so, not only is the world we live in the creation of God, but also the order we observe in the world was designed by God. For at the time of the creation of the world God implanted in it certain laws, laws of nature and laws of causality, by which it is to be governed. Philo, who first formulated this principle for all religious philosophers who were to follow him, calls it in Greek "the divine Logos"; and later medieval philosophers continue to call it their own Latin "*ratio divina*."

This is a sort of constitution which God Himself has drawn up for His own governance of the world. On the whole, God is conceived by most of the religious philosophers as a constitutional monarch who rules in accordance with the laws He designed for the world. But still they all agree that God, obedient to His own law though He is, has not abandoned His power nor His freedom. Should the good of His subjects demand it, He will upset the laws of nature which He has implanted in the world and produce what is called miracles.

Here again, Spinoza starts with a willingness to adopt the religious vocabulary and describe the relation of his God to the universe — the wholeness of it in relation to its parts from which it is inseparable and with which it is eternally coexistent — as a relation of cause and effect. For *cause*, in philosophic language, is one of those weasel words which may be used by different men in different senses. In ordinary speech, a *cause* is what brings about the existence of something. But in the philosophic language of Spinoza's time any kind of relation between two things, or even within one thing, any kind of relation between two distinguishable aspects of the thing, could be described as a causal relation. Especially was the term *cause* used as a description of the relation of the whole to the part.

But — and here the second "but" comes in — Spinoza is unwilling to admit that there is a God who is the *cause* of the world in the sense that He created it by will and design, so that if He willed it, there need have been no world, or there might have been a different kind of world; nor is Spinoza willing to admit that, once God created the world after a certain order, He can miraculously upset that order. The world as it now exists, as well as the order which we observe in it, is fixed, immutable, and inexorable; and it has so existed, without any change, from eternity.

For Spinoza, we must bear in mind, was an old-fashioned philosopher, who knew nothing of what we now call "evolution." He was in this respect more old-fashioned than the religious philosophers to whom he was opposed. In the case of religious philosophers, homiletical historians of religion may find in their vague descriptions of the process of creation certain adumbrations of evolution. But no homiletical historian of philosophy — even those who have discovered in Spinoza adumbrations of Marxian dialectics, Freudian psychology, and Einsteinian relativity — will be able to find in his conception of the eternally complete and fixed universe any traces of a theory of cosmic evolution.

Spinoza's description, then, of the wholeness of the universe in relation to its parts as *cause* was simply a concession to his opponents. It was justified only by the license exercised by philosophers in the use of the term *cause*, and also by his own disinclination to quarrel about words. But, having once expressed his willingness to describe his own God by the traditional term *cause*, Spinoza goes even further to express his willingness to describe Him as a cause in the various senses in which traditional philosophers described their God as *cause*. His wholeness of the universe is thus to Spinoza not only a mere *cause* but also a *first cause*, a *principal cause*, a *universal cause*, an *efficient cause*, an *essential cause*, an *immanent cause*, a *free cause*. However, in every one of these instances, he shows in what special sense he uses these terms. In some instances, he also shows how his use of these terms is even more justifiable than that of his opponents.

Spinoza's criticism of the traditional conceptions of the separability and causality of God — conceptions which, as fundamental principles of scriptural religious philosophy, were first formulated by Philo — led him to an examination of a philosophy which is quite the opposite of the philosophy of Philo — that is, the emanationist theory of Plotinus.

The philosophy of Plotinus may, indeed, be considered as the counterpart of the philosophy of Philo. Just as Philonism is a rationalization of Hebrew Scripture, so the Neoplatonism of Plotinus is a rationalization of pagan mythology; and, if the truth were known, it originated as a pagan reaction to Philonism. In opposition to Philonism, emanationism denies that God, either after the manner of a potter created the world from a pre-existent matter, or after the manner of a stage-magician created it out of nothing. Emanationism maintains instead that, after the manner of a spider which spins its web out of itself, God caused the world to emanate out of His own essence. Again in opposition to Philo, it maintains that this process of emanation is an eternal process and a necessary process. But then, while rejecting the Philonic belief in the separateness of God in the sense that He could exist without the world, it maintains His separateness in the sense of His being immaterial.

Here, again, Spinoza is willing to adopt the emanationist vocabulary and describe the relation between the wholeness of the universe and its parts as a process in accordance with which the parts flow from, or follow from, the whole. Logically, he sees no difference between the emanationist God, who coexists with the world from eternity and acts upon it as a necessary cause, from his own conception of God *as the wholeness of the universe*. He is even willing to describe his own God as the emanative cause of the universe. In fact, when he decided to build up his few religious heresies into an imposing system of philosophy, it was the system of emanation that he took as his model.

But — and here his third "but" comes in — Spinoza does not admit that his God is separated from the world in the sense that He is immaterial. He shows how, by the assumption of an immaterial God, there is no adequate explanation under the theory of emanation for the rise of matter. Of course, he was aware of the answer provided by the emanationists — in their theory of an intermediary mind as the immediate emanation from God and the immediate emanative source of matter. But he shows how the interposition of such an intermediary between God and matter fails to solve the difficulty, how furthermore it gives rise to new difficulties, and how in fact the emanationist theory is really nothing but a disguised form of the belief in creation out of nothing. He concludes, therefore, that if the relation between the wholeness of the universe and its parts is to be described in terms of emanation, then the wholeness cannot be described as immaterial.

Proceeding now to recast his own few simple views into a philosophic system modelled after that of emanationism, Spinoza tries to express the difference between these two systems — his own and emanationism — in technical terms. The technical terms which Spinoza uses for this purpose are *attribute*, *thought*, and *extension*.

Attribute is a term he borrows from the vocabulary of religious philosophy, where it was used as a description of the way we conceive of God and speak of Him in terms derived from His manifestation in the world. *Extension* and *thought* are terms used in the more fashionable vocabulary of Spinoza's own time for the old-fashioned terms "matter" and "form." And so he contrasts the emanationist view with his own by saying that to the emanationists God has only *the attribute of thought*, whereas to him God has both the *attribute of thought* and *the attribute of extension*.

Again, to the emanationists, whose God has only the *attribute of thought*, the immediate thing that follows from God is an intellect; to Spinoza, whose God has both the *attribute of thought* and the *attribute of extension*, the immediate thing that follows from God is twofold, an intellect and motion. These he describes, respectively, as the *infinite immediate mode of thought* and the *infinite immediate mode of extension*.

As in emanationism, all the particular things in the world are described by Spinoza as following from these two immediate infinite modes, and hence in their totality are described by him as mediate infinite modes or as "the face of the whole universe," which phrase, as we have said, he himself has coined out of reminiscent terms and expressions. Finally, from somewhere in that stockpile of philosophic terminology he dragged out the expressions "naturating nature" (*natura naturans*) and "naturated nature" (*natura naturata*), and used them as designations, respectively, of *substance* and *modes*.

Behind the imposing façade of Spinoza's philosophic system, with all its intricacies of design and vocabulary, there is thus a simple philosophic faith. Directly, this philosophic faith is presented in opposition to the traditional religious faith. But indirectly, as may be judged from certain expressions in Spinoza's correspondence, it is also aimed at the old Epicurean faith, which in his time was still the bugbear of both theologians and philosophers. In opposition both to the religious faith, which professed a belief in the creation of the world by the will of an eternal God, and to the Epicurean faith, which professed a belief in the emergence of the world out of the accidental collision of aimlessly drifting eternal atoms, Spinoza's philosophic faith protested that the world in its present form existed from eternity.

Again, in opposition to the religious faith, which saw in the order of the universe certain laws of causality which were implanted in it by the will of God, and which God by His will can miraculously upset — and in opposition also to the faith of the Epicureans, who saw in the order of the universe only an accidental equilibrium of stray forces, liable at any moment to be upset — this simple philosophic faith of Spinoza sees in the order of the universe certain eternally fixed laws of causality, with which all the apparently wayward behavior of particular things is indissolubly connected by an imperceptible chain of causes.

But then a question arose in the mind of Spinoza. How do we know that the Epicurean faith is mistaken? Perhaps, after all, the world is only a conglomeration of atoms which had come together by chance. Perhaps what appears to us as causal order is only the result of a chance equilibrium of atoms. Moreover, what guarantee have we that the order which has existed till now will continue to exist in the future?

When this question occurred to religious philosophers, they answered it by what is known as the proofs of the existence of God. The proofs used by them, with one exception, contain nothing new; they inherited them from pagan philosophers. On the whole, these proofs of the pagan philosophers fall into two classes.

Those philosophers who believed that all our knowledge is derived ultimately from sense perception maintained that the existence of God could be proved only indirectly from our various sensible perceptions of the world. This gave rise to those proofs for the existence of God which are known nowadays as the cosmological proofs, of which the best known is that syllogistic jingle, which begins with the premise, "All things that are in motion must be moved by some-thing." On the other hand, those who believed that some of our knowledge, indeed the most valid portion of it, is born within our own mind, maintained that the existence of God is a direct kind of knowledge within our own mind.

These two modes of proving the existence of God, invented by pagan philosophers, were adopted by later religious phi-losophers, though some of them rejected the second type of proof. But these later religious philosophers added a new kind of direct knowledge of the existence of God, namely, the historical revelation of God as recorded in Scripture, and the divine illumination which may be experienced by certain favored individuals. Moreover, in imitation of those proofs known to us as cosmological, the various assertions of the immediacy of our knowledge of the existence of God have in later days been resolved into syllogistic jingles which came to be known as the ontological proofs.

Here, again, Spinoza begins by admitting that the exist-ence of what he has already agreed to call God is a direct kind of knowledge within us, for Spinoza believed our mind is capable of generating knowledge of itself. But he refuses to admit that we can have a direct knowledge of God either by revelation or by divine illumination. Following in the footsteps of those who asserted a direct knowledge of the existence of God, he is not content with merely stating his profession of faith; he presents his profession of faith in the form of various syllogistic demonstrations, describing these demonstrations by the term *a priori*.

Altogether he advances three such *a priori* demonstrations. In one instance, he performs before our eyes the verbal trans-formation of an indirect proof of the existence of God, or what he calls an *a posteriori* demonstration, into a direct proof, or an *a priori* demonstration.

From a consideration of God, Spinoza passes on to a con-sideration of Man.

To religious philosophers, man as the crown of creation occupies a unique place in the universe. In this view, man's uniqueness does not consist in the mere fact that he possesses a soul; for, not only from the works of philosophers but also from their own Scripture, they gathered that other living beings also have a soul.

The singularity of man consisted in the fact that he had a special soul of special origin. Spinoza himself, in his book called *Cogitata Metaphysica*, which is really not a book but a scrapbook, alludes to the three theories of the origin of the human soul held by various religious philosophers. In technical language they are known as the theories of creation, pre-existence, and traducianism. In plain English they may be described, respectively, as the theory of custom-made souls, the theory of ready-made souls, and the theory of second-hand souls.

According to the custom-made theory, at the birth of each child God creates a soul especially for that child. According to the ready-made theory, at the time of the creation of the world God in His foresight created individual souls which in number and variety were sufficient to supply the need of all the future generations of men. These souls are kept in a place the exact name of which is variously given by various authorities who are expert in the knowledge of these matters. At each child's birth a soul suitable to his body is placed within him — though, judging by the great number of misfit souls in the world, one may infer that mistakes frequently occur. According to the second-hand theory of the soul, God, at the time of the creation of the world, created only one soul, and that is the soul of Adam. All our souls are only slices of the soul of our first ancestor, so remade as to fit our own peculiar bodies.

The common element in these three theories of the origin of the human soul — which is of philosophic interest to Spinoza — is that the human soul is of divine origin, and has been especially created by God apart from the body, so that even after it is placed in the body it continues to exist there as something apart from it.

As usual, Spinoza has no objection to adopting the vocabulary of his opponents and describing the human soul as being of divine origin. The technical vocabulary in which he has clothed his thought allows him to say that "the human mind is part of the infinite intellect of God." [1] In fact, this statement is so phrased as to allude to a medieval discussion of the nature of the divine origin of the soul. But — and here another "but" comes in — he does not admit that the soul is separable from the body.

Everything in the world, Spinoza argues, has a double aspect. In one respect, everything in the world may be looked upon as something simple and isolated. Looked upon in this way, everything in the world has only one simple mode of behavior. It is always in flux, constantly in a process of change: it is always ceasing to be what it is and becoming something else. Earlier philosophers called it matter, and matter was defined as extension. Spinoza, in his own technical vocabulary, calls it *extended thing*, or a *part of the infinite immediate mode of motion*, or a *finite mode of the attribute of extension*.

In another respect, everything in the world, however simple, is composed of parts and, however isolated, is part of something else. Looked upon in this way, everything in the world, in relation to itself, has a structure and, in relation to other things, has a function. Earlier philosophers called it form. But form is not one single thing. There is a hierarchy of forms. Some philosophers enumerated the several stages in the hierarchy of form by such general terms as cohesion, nature, soul, mind. Other philosophers, however, used a different kind of vocabulary and, instead of speaking of a hierarchy of forms and of everything as having a form, spoke of a hierarchy of souls and of everything as having a soul. Spinoza adopts this vocabulary and hence says, "all things have a soul

[1] *Ethics* II, 11, Corol.

(*omnia animata*)," adding immediately the qualifying phrase "in different degrees." [2]

And so, Spinoza argues, the human soul is only one of the degrees of soul which all things possess; and just as the cohesiveness, which is the soul of a clod of earth, or growth, which is the soul of a plant, is inseparable from the body of the stone or the plant, so is mind, which is the soul of man, inseparable from the body of man. In his own vocabulary, mind and body are respectively *finite modes* of God's attributes of *thought* and *extension*; and, just as in God these two attributes are united together, so are mind and body in man. Referring therefore to this argument of his, Spinoza concludes: "Hence we see not only that the human mind is united to the body, but also what is to be understood by the union of the mind and body." [3]

As a corollary of the conception of the soul as being of divine origin, and separate from the body, is the conception of its freedom.

On the whole, to religious philosophers man, though occupying a special position in the world, is still a part of nature, and his actions, like all natural actions in the world, are determined by certain laws of causality which are of divine design and implantation. There are no free actions in man, as there are no free motions in the world. Still there are certain exceptions. In the world, God may change the order of nature and create miracles; in man, the mind is endowed with a similar power to change the order of human nature and produce actions which are miraculously free. Philo, who was the first to formulate the philosophic basis of this kind of undetermined human freedom, says that God endowed the human mind with a proportion "of that free will which is His most peculiar possession and most worthy of His majesty," and that by this gift of free will the human mind "has been made to resemble God." [4] And both the miracles worked by God

---

[2] *Ethics* II, 13, Schol.   [3] *Ethics* II, 13, Schol.   [4] *Immut.* 10, 47-48.

in nature and the miraculous power of the freedom of the human mind are two forms of the selfsame providence by which God governs the world. What is the purpose of miracles? To protect man against the evils of the external forces of nature. What is the purpose of freedom? To protect man against the evil forces of his own nature.

Spinoza is willing to describe man as free. But he denies that his freedom is undetermined. To him, as there are no miracles in nature, so there is no miraculous freedom in human nature. Freedom is power, the power of reason by which man may control and guide the forces of his own nature, just as by the same power of reason he can control and guide the forces of external nature. Every conflict in man is looked upon by Spinoza as a conflict between two physical forces, which he calls by their old philosophic names, reason and emotion; and as in every conflict between two opposite physical forces, the stronger force will subdue the weaker. Man is called free only in the sense that by an increased knowledge of his own nature reason will grow in strength to overcome all the adverse forces of his emotions.

There is nothing miraculous about this kind of freedom. Referring to those who, like Philo, saw in human freedom an endowment of the human mind with a miraculous power by which it is made to resemble God, Spinoza observes that by the same token "they say that the mind can by its own strength create sensations or ideas which do not belong to things, so that in a measure they make it out to be a God." [5] It is doubtful whether Spinoza had a direct knowledge of Philo; but the Philonic view is also restated by Descartes when he says that free will "in a certain sense renders us like God in making us masters of ourselves." [6] By aiming directly at Descartes, Spinoza indirectly hit Philo.

Religion, to religious philosophers, was not only a truth,

[5] *Tractatus de Intellectus Emendatione* 60.
[6] *Les Passions de l'Ame* III, 152.

a way of knowing, but also a good, a way of living. To them God in His governance of the world, by His individual providence, has in His infinite wisdom not only endowed men with freedom but has also revealed to them laws of conduct by which, through the exercise of their freedom, they are guided to their destined good. These divinely revealed laws — it was insisted upon by the religious philosophers — were not the prescripts of an arbitrary ruler; they were based upon reason. In fact, they were the virtues which philosophers, in their fumbling way, were trying to discover by their own faulty reason as rules of conduct whereby men were to attain their highest good.

Here, again, Spinoza begins by saying "yes." Yes, he admits that the practical teachings of Scripture, unlike its intellectual teachings, contain some merit. But — and here another "but" comes in — he denies that they are divinely revealed, or that they are of the same nature as the virtues dealt with by the philosophers. They are the practical wisdom of simple-minded men, based upon their limited experience in a simple form of life.

And so in direct opposition to traditional philosophy, which presented its ethics in the form of a systematization of the teachings of the various philosophers interspersed with quotations of scriptural proof-texts, Spinoza reproduces the same systematization without the benefit of any supporting scriptural quotations. Following in the footsteps of Aristotle, the Stoics, and their successors, he defines the nature of the highest good, of happiness, and of virtue; and out of the writings of these philosophers he draws up a list of virtues and vices to take the place of the positive and negative commandments of religious legislation.

In addition to its being a truth, a way of knowing, and a good, a way of living, religion is also a promise, a way of attaining happiness.

The promise of happiness held out by religion, as Spinoza

sees it, is twofold: happiness in the present life and happiness in what is called the hereafter. Spinoza describes the happiness religion promises in this world by the phrase "*mentis acquiescentia*." An English translation of this phrase, partly literal and partly free, would be "peace of mind"; though, judging by the current lists of best-sellers, it would be more fashionable to translate it by "peace of soul." The God of traditional religion is not only the powerful architect of the universe and the wise lawgiver for mankind. He is also the great provider, the great comforter, the rock of salvation, the refuge in the day of evil. To man, burdened with trouble, old-time religion offers one sovereign remedy. "Cast thy burden upon the Lord, and He will sustain thee" (Ps. 55: 23/22); "Take my yoke upon you . . . and ye shall find rest unto your souls" (Matt. 11:29).

Again, in a way, Spinoza says "yes." He does not deny that religion offers consolation to the true believers. But — and here still another "but" comes in — there is a consolation of philosophy as there is a consolation of religion. Reason, he claims, can restore peace of mind, or peace of soul, without benefit of the soothing words of the Psalms or the Gospels. And he thus undertakes to prescribe philosophic remedies for the various ailments of the soul.

In a series of twenty propositions, Spinoza tells us how we can be happy though miserable. He tells us how we may overcome anxiety, fear, worry, desire, ambition, envy, disappointment, frustration, hatred, self-pity, and all the other innumerable ills that stem from the emotions. In the past generations, readers of Spinoza saw in these propositions a distillation of the cumulative wisdom of the ages, wisdom writ large in the form of proverbs in the pages of copy-books. Readers of today see in them adumbrations of the newly discovered science of the mind, its traumas and its therapies. Spinoza himself presents them in profound technical language as a philosophic cathartic for the emotions, as a metaphysic for bilious souls.

The promise held out by religion for happiness in the hereafter is the promise of immortality. Here, too, we may gather from Spinoza's discussion that, on the one hand, while he is willing to admit that the soul is immortal — or eternal, as he prefers to call it, following one of Cicero's usages — on the other hand, his own conception of its immortality is of a somewhat special kind. But what he means exactly by that special kind of immortality is not quite clear. Let us try to find out.

At the time of Spinoza there were three distinct views of immortality. Each of these views has a long and complicated history, and a variety of subtly distinguishable aspects. But for our present purpose we shall describe them briefly in their main outlines.

The first view may be described as that of individual immortality by the grace of God. According to this view, the soul is a creation of God and begins its existence as an individual entity. As a creation of God, the soul by its own nature cannot be eternal, for only God is eternal. By His infinite grace and power, however, God confers immortality upon the souls of certain individuals as a reward for their conduct during their lifetime. Accordingly, it is only the souls of those who are stamped as righteous that are immortal; the souls of those who are stamped as wicked are annihilated.

This, on the whole, is a conception of immortality to which, theoretically, all religious philosophers would subscribe; though, historically, many of them preferred to see the wicked eternally punished rather than utterly annihilated. But the difference between utter annihilation and eternal punishment is only a matter of taste, not a matter of theory. The belief in eternal punishment does not exclude the possibility of utter annihilation. In fact, certain theologians, learned in these matters, speak of both eternal punishment and utter annihilation and interpret either one in terms of the other.

The second view may be described as that of universal immortality by nature. According to this view, the soul does not begin its existence as an individual entity, but as part of a universal soul of which each man gets a portion. Since the universal soul is homogeneous, all portions of it distributed among individual men are alike in nature. It is only through their contact with different bodies that the souls of different individuals appear to act differently. But this contact of souls with bodies leaves no permanent effect upon them. As soon as the bodies die, the accidental individual differences between their respective souls disappear. The souls of all men, in their original undifferentiated nature, return to the universal soul and, reabsorbed within it, retain no trace of their erstwhile temporarily acquired accidental individuality.

The third view is a modification of the one just described. It may be called individual immortality by nature. This view, too, assumes that there is a universal soul, of which the soul of every individual human being is an undifferentiated portion, and that whatever individuality it displays during its existence in the body is owing to its contact with that body. Yet such contact, especially as it results in the knowledge of the external world, and of what lies beyond that world, leaves upon the soul a permanent mark. It essentially transforms the nature of the soul; it changes it into something distinct and individual. This distinctness and individuality, by the eternal order of nature, is retained by the soul even after it departs from the body. It is as an individualized soul that it returns to its native source, the universal soul. It is not reabsorbed by it; it only finds shelter in it. The universal soul is a sort of heaven, to which the disembodied souls of philosophers, if not of saints, return in their naked spirituality to enjoy bliss for evermore in the presence of God.

These are the three views with which Spinoza, we assume, started his speculation concerning immortality. He must have examined each one of them, trying to find out which one he could accept without involving himself in contradictions.

The first view he must have found himself compelled to

reject at once, for it was contradictory to his entire conception of God and of the human soul.

The second view he must have thought, at first, he could accept. For in the philosophic system he had built up after the model of the emanationist philosophy there is a universal soul which he calls the infinite intellect of God; and of that soul the human soul is, as he has said, a part; and that part of the infinite intellect of God is certainly not annihilated with the death of man: it is reabsorbed in the source whence it came. For with his denial of creation out of nothing, Spinoza also denied the destruction of anything into nothing. Quite consistently, therefore, he could express himself as willing to accept the immortality of the soul in the sense of the universal immortality of the soul.

But after some reflection Spinoza decided, we presume, to reject this kind of immortality. He would only stultify himself, he reasoned, if he were to speak of a universal immortality of the soul, when, on the basis of his own philosophy, he could also speak of a universal immortality of the body. For in his own philosophy there is a universal body as there is a universal soul, and both are inseparably united, and of that universal body the individual human body is a part, and, upon the death of man, just as his soul is reabsorbed in the universal soul, so is his body reabsorbed in the universal body. What sense is there in speaking of the immortality of the soul unless the soul, unlike the body, in its reabsorption in the universal soul retains a certain kind of individuality which is not found in the body in its reabsorption in the universal body?

And so Spinoza must have come to examine the third view of immortality. With regard to this view he must have found that there is nothing in his philosophy to preclude the assumption that, by the eternal order of nature, that portion of the infinite intellect of God which constitutes the human mind acquires, through its experience in life, a certain distinctness and individuality which remains with it even after death when it is reunited with that infinite intellect of God whence it originally came. If he were asked how that happened, he would answer that it was so determined by the eternal order of nature. For it must be borne in mind that the eternal order, to Spinoza, was a sovereign explanation for everything inexplicable, just as the will of God was to the Philonic religious philosophers. Nothing is impossible in an eternally ordered world, such as is conceived by Spinoza, just as nothing is impossible in a world governed by the will of God, such as is conceived by Philonic philosophers. It is only in a world where everything new must arise in a process of evolution that certain things may be conceived as impossible.

Having found this third view of immortality not inconsistent with his philosophy, Spinoza accepted it. The terms he uses in his restatement of it reflect exactly the terms commonly used in the descriptions of this view. It is not in all its faculties, Spinoza maintains, that soul is immortal, for the faculties of imagination and memory are destroyed with the body.[7] This is quite in accordance with the third view of immortality. Still, he continues, "the human mind cannot be absolutely destroyed with the body, but something of it remains which is eternal";[8] and that something of it which remains eternal, he explains, is conditioned upon the acquisition of knowledge of a certain kind. This, again, is in accordance with the third view of immortality. He then concludes, "The essence of the mind consists of knowledge . . . therefore the more things the mind knows . . . the greater is that part of it which remains."[9] This, once more, is in accordance with the explanation given by the exponents of the third view of immortality for the individual differences between immortal souls.

And so here again Spinoza begins by admitting that there is individual immortality of the soul. But — and here the last

[7] *Ethics* V, 21.
[8] *Ibid.*, 23.
[9] *Ibid.* V, 38, Demonst.

"but" comes in — this individual immortality belongs to man not by grace but by nature.

Yet, while Spinoza's assertion of individual immortality is not inconsistent with his philosophy, it does not necessarily follow from it. It is a gratuitous principle; it is an expression of faith rather than of reason. On the rational basis of his philosophy he could have said — just as he has said in his discussion of God, of the human soul, and of the revealed law — yes, I am willing to use the word immortality and use it even in the sense of individual immortality, but I do not mean by it the immortality of man's soul; I mean by it the immortality of man's achievements. In fact, this is exactly what most students of Spinoza take to be the meaning of his statements about the eternity of the soul. But while Spinoza might have spoken in this vein, he does not in fact so speak; and there is no indication that he meant his writings to be treated as divinely inspired sacred texts which pious readers were constantly to modernize by constantly giving them allegorical interpretations.

And so, while Spinoza's conception of immortality betrays no logical inconsistency of thought, it betrays an inconsistency of mood. Departing from the method followed by him in his speculations about God, about the soul, or the revealed law, he is here willing to accept more than the mere use of a term; he is willing to accept a certain belief.

This change of mood is to be noticed also in his attempt to cite scriptural proof-texts for his belief in immortality. Such citation marks a departure from his general practice in the *Ethics*. Nowhere in the *Ethics* does he quote scriptural verses in support of his view. And yet here, after developing his views on the individual immortality of the soul, he tries, almost like Maimonides or Thomas Aquinas, to tell us how his conception of immortality is in agreement with that of Scripture. He describes the state of immortality by such New Testament terms as salvation, liberty, regeneration, and blessedness, all of which consists in the love of God, or union with Him, and then concludes, "This love or blessedness is called Glory in the sacred writings." [10] In fact, this last statement of Spinoza's is a paraphrase of the following statement in St. Thomas: "Hence this blessedness is many times described as glory in the sacred writings: thus it is said (Ps. 149:5), 'The Saints exult in glory.' " [11] Similarly, Abraham Ibn Ezra, who is quoted by Spinoza in his *Tractatus Theologico-Politicus*, commenting upon the verse of the Psalm quoted by St. Thomas, says: "Let the saints exult in that glory which awaits them, namely, in the eternal existence that they shall enjoy, referring thereby to the eternal existence of their souls, or to what is called the hereafter."

Still further evidence for this change of mood is to be found in the new kind of opponent whom Spinoza visualizes in his discussion of immortality. As I have said, the *Ethics* is a critique of the philosophy of certain unnamed opponents. The opponents visualized throughout the *Ethics* are the religious philosophers. Now the opponent visualized in his discussion of immortality, as may be judged from the context, is a religious heretic, Uriel Acosta, who died when Spinoza was a boy of about fifteen. Eight years before Spinoza's birth Acosta became known as a heretic through the publication of a work in which he denied the immortality of the soul, showing that there was no such belief in Scripture. This book evoked a great deal of opposition, which continued for many years after its publication. In Spinoza's discussion of immortality there are several passages directed against Uriel Acosta.

What brought about this change of mood in Spinoza cannot be exactly determined. If we were writing historical fiction, we might invent all kinds of situations to explain this change. As historians, trying to reconstruct the true doctrine of Spinoza, all we can say is that Spinoza, despite all his philosophizing, felt, even as you and I, the need of the consolation of this belief.

[10] *Ethics* V, 36, Schol. [11] *Cont. Gent.* III, 63.

The picture which I have drawn of Spinoza in his relation to religion is not the picture with which we are familiar. Spinoza is daring, but he introduces no novelty. His daring consists in overthrowing the old Philonic principles which by his time had dominated the thought of European religious philosophy for some sixteen centuries. But in overthrowing these principles, all he did was to reinstate, with some modification, the old principles of classical Greek philosophy. That is what he did in dealing with the concepts of God, the soul, freedom, ethics, and immortality, though, in the case of immortality, he follows a medieval variation of the Platonic conception of immortality.

Perhaps this is all one could expect of Spinoza or of any other philosopher. For on all these religious issues there are only two alternatives. One was stated in the Hebrew Scripture, and the other in the various writings of Greek philosophers. Thereafter, the great question in the history of religious philosophy was whether to follow the one or the other, or to combine the two. And in the history of religious philosophy, so conceived, two figures are outstanding, Philo and Spinoza. Philo was the first to combine the two; Spinoza was the first to break up that combination.